DARK S
THE LOON

Ben Lee Almond

chipmunkapublishing
the mental health publisher

Ben Lee Almond

Published by
Chipmunkapublishing
PO Box 6872
Brentwood
Essex CM13 1ZT
United Kingdom

http://www.chipmunkapublishing.com

Chipmunkapublishing gratefully acknowledge the support of Arts Council England.

DARK SIDE OF THE LOON

INDEX

32. A BILLION MINDS
33. A DAZE FEROCIOUS
34. BLING BLING BLA
35. PROS AND CONS
36. HELL A CUBIC CELL
37. STEAL THE SHOW
38. EYE SPY
39. DEATH OR JAIL
40. A POSITIVE POEM
41. THE GNARLED TREE
42. ALREADY DEAD
43. EYES WIDE SHUT
44. RATIONAL MINDS WON'T BELIEVE
45. I LOVE YOU
46. A LIQUID BLACK
47. SANDMAN'S LAIR
48. MR. BLAIR WOTCHA SMOKIN'
49. CE 81 DRAW
50. OPEN SESAME SPELLCASTER
51. DRY YOUR EYES MATE
52. INSECURITY OPPOSITES ATTRACT
53. TEARS ARE HOLY
54. ANCIENT WHISPERS
55. COCKTAIL RAMPAGE
56. ABOLISHMENT
57. BOOK HAT STONES
58. THE EARTH AND THE FIRE
59. A SNITCH IN TIME SAVES CRIME
60. DIRTY DEED
61. FINDER'S KEEPERS
62. A BIRO DEPLETION
63. A SECRET PLACE
64. SWEET DREAMS
65. BO LOZOFF

DARK SIDE OF THE LOON

Ben Lee Almond

DARK SIDE OF THE LOON

To all the people who understood and helped me
along the way
Thank you for your inspiration

Ben Lee Almond

DARK SIDE OF THE LOON

NEW LIFE REVITALISED

Fed up and bored, ain't nowt to do
Nine years old and I'm sniffing glue
Petrol thinners, boot polish too
Young and foolish I didn't have a clue
Got deeper in, two months past
You could catch my lips round a tin a gas
What went wrong you had to ask
Mushy season came and yeah, I had a blast

When I hit eleven, well I hit the weed
Bye to the solvents, my mind was freed
How wrong was I when along came speed
Doing it for fun turned into a need
I craved for the buzz and wanted the feeling
A boost of the ego I started dealing
Plenty of cash, a great big stash
Half the town was smoking my ash

Started growing skunk, you know how it goes
And all the profits were going up my nose
A teenager taught me how to wash the coke
Sniffing is shit you wanna try a smoke?
I said OK I'm an easy led bloke
I should've said no and it's not a joke
Instantly addicted off just one puff
Wired every day I couldn't get enough

Couldn't get to sleep, couldn't settle down
After a while I started tootin' brown
High all day, sedated at night
My body was fucked I had no fight
Rooting on the floor, did I drop a little bit?

Ben Lee Almond

Looking in the kitchen where I wasn't smoking it
It fries your brain, fucks with your mind
Can't see reality it turns you blind

I needed sex I wanted it now
Didn't care why didn't care how
Sleeping with the pros just coz I could
Wanted it all I was only young blood
Sex on the brain frustrated in pain
And all because of crack cocaine
Which led me to a heroin addiction
A physical, mental, terrible affliction
I owed the dealer two ton fifty
Came knocking on my door looking shifty
I went out to see, what's the matter
He swung for me so I picked up a hammer
I struck him quick, hard as I could
Hit his head on the floor there was lots of blood
He got up and said I can't see
I thought OK that'll do for me

Big bad gangster grassed to the cops
I did time in jail where time just stops
Doing my rip doing a rattle
I cut my arms but I won the battle
I wrote to a girl whilst clutching on straws
She saw my pain and showed me the cause
The craving stopped the aching went away
She told me the truth I was led astray

Seven and a half months on remand
Self-defence didn't have it planned
Section eighteen with intent
My time in jail was time well spent

DARK SIDE OF THE LOON

I learned to write words properly
It gave my mind some sanctuary
Stopped self harming, don't take drugs
Don't hang around with nasty thugs

But the side effects of a poisoned mind
Was schizophrenia I did find
Packed off to the psychiatric ward
Couldn't get out, I got real bored
The drugs had warped reality
They took me to insanity
The floor was soft the sky was hard
I thought I was the new age God

I got better and reconnected
From the world of drugs I disconnected
Said I couldn't do it, now they're surprised
They see new life revitalised

Ben Lee Almond

RAMBLING VOICES AND DARK THOUGHTS

In the corner of my mind voices are rambling
Dark thoughts, disease, brain cells trampling
Lucifer's curse I put it down to bad blood
A wave of demons a ferocious flood

Spirits in limbo lost in my head
Listening to them they seem half dead
Nowhere to go but something to find
They need to cross over but fumble blind

Frustrated and nasty they vent anger on me
Showing me images I don't want to see
Death and castration, suffering and pain
Burning and scalding like acid rain

Gnawing, chewing, chopping and twisting
Severe agony the whole body blistering
Engulfed forever in a freezing fire
The worst feeling on earth torture, dire

Negativity and darkness rotting flesh
Solid brick walls and wire mesh
Taking over my body without consent
A violent rampage with a destructive intent

DARK SIDE OF THE LOON

FULL BOWL

Just imagine peace and love and lots of mega fun
Is it really hard to think that heavens in the sun?
Through the fields of space you'll get there when
you die
Or if you got life wrong you're born again to cry

Zion is the way; we'll all get there in the end
You've got to know the key, its no good to pretend
Faith in God and religion lends a hand
The centre of a star this is the Promised Land

Moons and planets first you'll see how they all
formed
Allah's magic works from the time the first man
yawned
A most merciful creation, life and death to all
See we're all equal playing with the very same ball

The power of the Lord touches all the same
Hostile minds burn out for they play a very sad
game
The universe is vast but small to divine power
Everlasting bliss bringing light to the darkest hour

Open your heart, your mind, body and soul
God will take care of you; He will fill up your bowl

Ben Lee Almond

MENACE TO SOCIETY

Its so lame things can never be the same
Guns and ammunition play a crazy game
Uzi nine millimetre gun, ho, bullet eater
AK47 a blasting firework repeater

Smith and western a painful lesson
Gang warfare a population recession
Cock the hammer, a mouth full of lead
Bodies lined in chalk with a hole in the head

Too many lives we are losing
We are on a power and ego proving
Media and films influencing death
From the end of a barrel taking innocent breath

Pistol whipping, angry, stupid and flipping
Opening fire without a care, man you're tripping
Chaos and fury, thoughts of blasting a hole
Death has come early to the victims, mind, body
and soul

Trigger-happy mad men doing a diseases job
Killing off brothers' quick style, leaving the rest of
the family to sob
A menace to society, guns are a man made
invention
We seriously need a cure; it's too late for
prevention

DARK SIDE OF THE LOON

RUSSIAN ROULETTE

E's are shit they just make you feel rough
If you're experiencing after affects that's just
fucking tough
Nobody forced you mate; you did it on your own
Is it really worth it when you begin to moan?
You've lost all your belongings coz you're proper
wasted
These are the strongest E's that you have ever
tasted

Your eyesight's going squiggly you've got blurry
vision
Drinking beer and taking pills is a crazy bad
decision
You think you're cool so decide to take one more
Pushing your mind to the limit, collapsing on the
floor
Laid down on your back, choking on sick
Half way in a coma, you need some help real quick

The night's been cut short. the hospital now you're
going
The boats sinking fast you better start fucking
rowing
Nobody dares tell the doctor exactly what's gone on
Why you took that many. you shouldn't of even took
one
You've had the wrong diagnosis they think you've
had a fit
Your friends didn't say a word they mustn't give a
shit

Ben Lee Almond

So what's this feeling of ecstasy now that you're a
cabbage?
Eating through a straw the pills have done their
damage
Silly ain't it really, you was only after fun
But you were playing Russian roulette with a fully
loaded gun

DARK SIDE OF THE LOON

PYRAMIDS

Be careful of the ever-watching eye
God doesn't need satellites in the sky
His magical power runs much deeper
Day or night he'll comfort the weeper

The weather is his, the mountains and seas
Creatures great and small, the birds the bees
All the planets, the stars the moon
How else could you see flowers in bloom?

Books and angels, Prophets and prayer
Allah alone sits on the high chair
Merciful and kind, knower of all
One God and he's on the ball

Sharing power with none, no wife, no son
He created everything, the future to come
The wonders of the world were made by his hand
All of the oceans, all of the land

So worship Allah only him you should pray
The compassionate Lord five times a day
But if you're a sinner and no sense of guilt
You'll suffer slave labour; it's how the pyramids
were built

Ben Lee Almond

NEW WORLD ORDER

The hospital staff just doesn't understand
Mental health patients are in a foreign land
Upset, angry, frustrated and confused
Some of these people were violently abused

Dark thoughts, nasty voices, brain running too high
Cuts upon the arms, this is a visible cry
Psychosis, schizophrenia, bi polar disorder
Get with the program; it's a new world order

Bereavement, rape, multi personality
Sectioned off, welcome to my reality
Medication, food, patience and time
Forceful injection without a crime

Impending doom these flowers don't bloom
Spending most of the day in the smoking room
Anxiety, paranoia, stress and strain
Mental torture, suffering and pain

Very claustrophobic, a need to get out
They won't let you go if you scream and shout
Addict turning violent in need of crazy brown
Before he does damage the staff all pin him down

Refusing to take tablets an injection in the bum
I've seen too much I want the leaving day to come
Salvation lies within this I'm sure
But we still need prevention and a fast acting cure

DARK SIDE OF THE LOON

A WILL TO KILL

I'm crazy in the brain, needing a solution
I need to dump this psychotic pollution
Section off another institution
Viscous voices, a nasty delusion

Dark thoughts, disease, mind corruption
Boxed in maze with no instruction
Ripping into my soul, a violent intrusion
Diluting my blood in a reality confusion

Sanctuary torn, oblivion being born
This mental affliction, doesn't even warn
A virus burning, destruction yearning
Pain and suffering is all I'm learning

Born snapping, beating and whacking
Needles in my nerves, spine column cracking
Cuts, slits, smashed to bits
In this world nothing fits

Putrid sweat, always in debt
Holocaust dreams, a bomb threat
Scorched by acid, nothing's placid
Death and dissection, cruelty massive

Slashing and tearing, torture preparing
Teeth knocked out, I've lost my bearing
Please understand, I'm uncontrollably ill
It's not my fault; I've got a will to kill

Ben Lee Almond

BROWN DISEASE

Heroin hell a baron land
An overdose needle in hand
White as a ghost, lips all blue
I warned you son, it's no good for you

Now you need help, you're dying real quick
You're on your back choking on sick
In the corner of your eye you see a man with a
hood
The grim reapers come for heroin blood

No going back you're in sin city
No heroin in hell, what a pity
So who's gonna help a smack head in pain?
Yourself is the answer, stop playing the game

Black death nothing, this is the brown disease
Killing off thousands with a frightening ease
Laying the dead out all skin and bones
When there's a drought you'll hear haunting groans

Your family can't believe you're wasting away
You're signing a death warrant day by day
So listen up and listen real hard
Think of your kids, give drugs the red card

DARK SIDE OF THE LOON

I AM THE SKY

The sky was dark the sea was rough
I whistled down the wind

The earth shook, the lightening struck
I whistled down the wind

The sun scorched, thunder bellowed
I whistled down the wind

The trees rocked, the rain poured
I whistled down the wind

The tornado screamed, the storm blew
I whistled down the wind

The volcano tremored, the hurricane roared
I whistled down the wind

I realised that I am the sky
The whistle and the wind

Ben Lee Almond

SOMETHING'S MISSING

The ocean has lost its wave
My soul has lost its crave
The sun has lost its rays
The weeks have missing days

The moon has lost its shine
The water won't turn to wine
The stars have lost their glow
I will never again see snow

Weak and frail, locked up in jail
No salvation from the Holy Grail
A wandering mind lost in time
Lots of criminals, lots of time

DARK SIDE OF THE LOON

WAY BEYOND THE STARS

Way beyond the stars
Where mans' eyes ne'er been
There lies the most beautiful place
Only Allah's eyes have seen

In the outer realms of infinity
In a universe so immense
A lake of tranquillity, a sea of dreams
A power so intense

Every second one is born
A shelter for the dead
And have faith in the oneness
Gods counting every head

Peace and serenity
An island in the sun
Welcome to the afterlife
Love and blissful fun

Ben Lee Almond

GOD'S EXPERIMENT

A splinter in the mind, a window with a smear
Psychotic schizophrenia, to see it's all too clear
Puzzles for the eyes, a thorn in the brain
Forgive me heavenly father if I begin to complain
You've burdened me with a disease that doesn't
have a cure
What sort of a god are you? Your love is supposed
to be pure

Why have you cursed my thoughts condemned my
head with voices?
Locked me up in hospital where I haven't got any
choices
Stripped me of dignity you've taken me to hell
Left me in the lurch like a skunk leaves a smell

Poisoning my inner feelings darkening my every
thought
Senseless suffering and pain are the lessons I'm
being taught
I'm cold and all alone I wish I'd never been born
No light, no salvation, my faith is being torn
You've sentenced me to negativity, a terrible
affliction
You've become my drug dealer; I've a monstrous
tablet addiction

Impending doom brings a violent hallucination
Death and destruction without an explanation
An endless abyss of depression fading into space
I'm your experiment, God, look into this twisted face
My will is cut to ribbons my heart can't live anymore

DARK SIDE OF THE LOON

So why should I worship a God whose put my mind
to war?

Ben Lee Almond

MATRIX

The stakes are high, the chips are low
To heroin hell, I see you're gonna go
Bye- bye bag head an infinity of pain
Speed and cocaine too, they play the same game

Matrix on the mind you're very easy to spot
Roaming dead on your feet, as though you've lost
the plot
The good in the world, who have seen the light,
can't believe their eyes
Because they've seen these devil drugs darkening
our children's skies

Needles strewn in the yards, disease paradise
Does it take your children's turn for you to realize
Ok, I admit it; I had a toot of crack
But believe me son I went to hell and back

Jail in the end for going off my head
Turning psychotic, mouth frothing, then to a
hospital bed
A mind twist, an overdose, shouldn't have gone
down that road
Fed up and poorly, weak and bored and now on a
psycho ward

I was sizzling my brain, playing a deadly game
And in the end I was the only one to blame
I know my words seem harsh, stern and very clear
But you can banish evil drugs and abolish any fear

DARK SIDE OF THE LOON

ECHO HEAD

Voices, voices go away
I'll meditate, I'll even pray
Nasty little words, whispers in my head
In the smoke lounge, in my bed

The doors always locked no fuckin' key
Please dear god, talk to me
Going real mad there's no escape
The daily madness all this rape

Dead spirits come won't leave me be
Insanity's reality don't you see
A lunatic ward I feel real bad
So I just chit and chat to me dead dad

Talking to the echo's in the corner of my mind
And in the darkness I'm fumbling blind
Psychiatric units been to 'em all
I heard the cry I heard the call

I can listen to humanity
Solve all the problems peacefully

Ben Lee Almond

OIL BURNER

You're under threat if you live in Iraq
You're under threat if ya skin is black
You're under threat if you wear a Muslim hat
You're under threat, you're under attack

We used to work with the Taliban
To get Russia out of Afghanistan
Well treat you worse than the Ku Klux Klan
Well steal your oil coz we don't give a damn

Fuck with us well bomb you free
With back to front insanity
Making wars to suit our cause
We are God and king and laws

Burning and looting claiming liberation
Bombing and shooting on false information
What d'ya expect we answer to none
Don't care for life where I'm from

Sad but true that's how it is
Stealing oil yeah that's our biz
Only bothered for the pipeline coarse
Blitzkrieg tactics and no remorse

It's futile to pray so get out the way
This is the mentality of the U.S.A

DARK SIDE OF THE LOON

PICU

Your mind melting scorched by pain
Dark thoughts disease an infected brain
A slipping soul, dark evil voices
Battering your will giving nasty choices
Electric shock smashed with a rock
You need to give this affliction a mental block

Caged in and trapped, a claustrophobic nightmare
A maze for the mind, a hellish stare
Hot and cold sweats, shaking bones
Drug addicts making awful moans
Sectioned off can't hide or escape
You can't run from the fiery rape

Your own fear comes true here
You're on a collision course and you can't steer
Stuck in reality you've lost your sanity
Crazy in the head, this is normality
They're spying on you; you think it's true
Paranoid and anxious depressed and blue

Problems, sins, psychotic grins
Just stick 'em in the loony bins
Can't get out can't do a damn thing?
Useless and damaged, a phone with no ring
Angry and frustrated, twisted and confused
A raging war you're battered and bruised

Ben Lee Almond

THE A TEAM

If I was asked to play Russian roulette
I'd take that gun without any sweat
See I found God he takes care of me
And as from now, we'll always be
Friends forever together we've smiled
For he is the father and I am his child

DARK SIDE OF THE LOON

DILLY DALLY

Why you dally
At the waterside
Sooner or later
You will be swept by the tide
Once chained to the world
Now set free
Natural and pure
Like the motion of the sea

Ben Lee Almond

ARE POPPIES INNOCENT?

My mum loves poppies but I hate smack
This country's on its knees, well off track
The youth don't know they're under attack
Tough love and knowledge is what they lack

A one way ticket to psychotic madness
All your days full of sadness
The opium God controls your mind
Twisting the senses making you blind

In a silver caldron cooking up death
Mixing up an overdose with prescription meth
Washing it down with whiskey and beer
You'll take owt when you ain't no fear

Your teeth are black you really smell
Catch 22 this heroin hell
Aching like fuck if you don't get a hit
You need to do a rattle if you give a shit

Your head gets hot but ya body's gonna freeze
It's the way it works this brown disease
A nice flower but don't be fooled
Mother natures sadistic and cruel

So innocent poppy agent of the devil
I'll educate the youth and put them on the level

DARK SIDE OF THE LOON

ROSEHILL TURF

Across the vast abyss of time
Warlords used the art of rhyme
A curse a potion unchangeable spell
Each ruler casting people to hell

The skill of merging words together
Power crazed controlling the weather
Voodoo witchcraft black magic science
Immortal soul, death, defiance

To be the best is the eternal quest
The powers that be want someone who's blessed
So I say I've walked the trail
I've seen the light and drank from the grail

Bermuda triangle been through it twice
I'm the best rhymer it feels so nice
A conquering king here to inspire
A fearsome Aries a burning fire

A lunar event heaven sent
I'm taking over with God's consent
A star, a moon, always in tune
Resurrection time and not a minute too soon

An Easter day birth on Rosehill turf
Lyrical sanctuary all over mother earth

Ben Lee Almond

SADISTIC FLOWER

Dirty black nails and hair full o' grease
It's easy to see who's got the brown disease
You stick out a mile like a night fire
Roaming around with an uncontrollable desire

Lying, cheating, thieving, playing dirty tricks
Burning all your bridges just to get ya next fix
You do it on your own don't need encouragement
But you keep forgetting ya body needs nourishment

You're a homing missile with a powder craze
And now you're stuck in a heroin maze
Skins barely hanging on ya skeleton frame
It's your own fault for playing the game

A cist and a virus from injecting death
This dusty dirt's gonna take ya last breath
A blood clot forming a lot of track marks
You're in the deep end swimming with sharks

Tooting off the foil just to get straight
The grim reapers waiting at your front gate
Digging too deep and a bad infection
Hospital again under doctor's inspection

Black death nothing this is heroin power
It yearns for cultivation, this sadistic flower
Searching for a hit you're a bag rat lusting
Not the type of people to be trusting

Handbag snatcher, finger thrusting
Robbing old ladies is proper disgusting

DARK SIDE OF THE LOON

So what should we do about this cancer?
Educate our children must be the answer

Ben Lee Almond

I'M ALWAYS HERE

Take my hand when you feel pain
Take my hand when you feel grief
Take my hand when you feel sorrow
Have faith and have belief

Take my hand when you feel down
Take my hand when you are shamed
Take my hand when they are laughing
And you are the one they blamed

Take my hand when you're upset
Take my hand when you cry
Take my hand when you're lonely
Or if you need an alibi

Take my hand when nobody cares
Take my hand when you feel bitter
Take my hand in any circumstance
And when nothing seems to glitter

Take my hand and start to cheer
Take my hand and dry up the tears
Take my hand and let go of fear
I'm God and I'm always here

DARK SIDE OF THE LOON

AFRICAN QUEEN

I've been searching all my life
For a jewel of blood and flesh
Queen of queens to be my wife
New, unique and fresh

Earth and fire all inter-twined
A superlative effect
A perfect match, two of a kind
Built on pure respect

The only dark between us two
Is the colour of skin and eyes
But you and you and only you
Perfectly match my wishful cries

Ben Lee Almond

EASTER DAY

I'm a searcher, I seek the Holy Grail
I've travelled far followed many a trail
I've looked down I've looked up
It's nowhere to be seen this magic cup

I think it's just one big mystery
A make believe untruthful history
East, south, north and west
Proclaimer, I put you to the test

I'll drink from yours we'll see the truth
Because Christ's grail gives eternal youth
Day and night sundown to sunrise
I'd been thinking and what a nice surprise

I found that cup coz I'm a sleuth
So listen up here's your proof
After meditation whilst in pray
I remembered my birth on Easter day

I am Christ out of many I drink
Taste mine and see what you think
Eternal youth do your inspection
My magic is on the day of resurrection

DARK SIDE OF THE LOON

VIOLENT TIMES AND VIKING CRIMES

We're all living in violent times
The government committing Viking crimes
My eyes are open, I see the signs
So I'm going to keep spitting these political rhymes
Mr. Blair is an arrogant fool
Using race and fear as a political tool

ID cards and retina scanning
A small fraction of the madness he's planning
Guns, drugs and oil, who is the dealer
Blair's bum boy, the free worlds leader
Killing thousands in a democratic rush
While our primeminister hides behind a Bush

Targeting pensioners and the poor and needy
Food for oil, man...that's just greedy
Using lives as bargaining chips
Misleading information, lies from your lips
Limbless soldiers, returning from the war
Grieving mothers, queuing at your door

Come on Bush and Blair, where's your sensibility
A hundred thousand dead, we call for accountability
Do your dreams at night, give birth to anguished
souls
Are your thoughts of suicide bombers, from ages
one to old?
If someone killed you both, it wouldn't be a shame
Just two less bullyboys taken out the game

MAGIC 27

Wake up people
This can be paradise town
Where the air is clean, streets are safe
And nobody wears a frown

Drugs would get a red card
Cast off into exile
Just piece, love and spirit
For a thousand million miles

Money's not a problem
For we know it grows on trees
Everybody's got one
With a thank you and a please

Children happily playing
On the park and on the street
One and all have a glow
From their head down to their feet

Multiculturalism triumphant
Serenity now the way
The whole world meditating
Every single day

A dawning of a new age
This is surely heaven
And all along all it took
Was that magic 27

DARK SIDE OF THE LOON

JUST FOR YOU

You're a diamond, an angel shining bright
You're a shooting star on a purple night
The most amazing creation I've ever seen
The best destination I've ever been

My love for you is like bees' love for honey
What we share you can't buy with money
I can honestly say you're daddy's girl
My sweet child my precious pearl

Passionate about you from the start
You'll always have a place deep in my heart
Your eyes a lagoon a crystal paradise
Much more fresh than the clearest skies

I hold you in my arms you're a soft cloud
Your intellect shows and it makes me proud
Ill teach you things my dad taught me
We'll even plant an Almond tree

You're a rare flower always blooming
Don't forget you're my little moomin
I'll tell you things to make you smile
To see such bliss it's all worthwhile

So if you feel down or when you feel blue
Remember these words they're just for you

Ben Lee Almond

WHO AM I?

I created rain, wind, snow and sleet
I gave you fingers and the toes on your feet
I made the sky the stars way up high
The sun, the moon, day and night

Creatures great and small, North and South Pole
Everything in existence no orders too tall
Suspended animation is my creation
All colours, all creeds, every nation

Diamonds, ruby's, emeralds and oil
Fire, air, water and even soil
Birds and bees, I made the trees
Waterfalls and grass mountains and seas

Gold, silver, all things metal
I gave defence to the stinging nettle
I'm the divine power over all I tower
I create miracles in the neediest hour

I'm one on my own, sitting the high throne
Intricate, unfathomable, I'm one you can't clone
I gave the wizards every single spell
I created heaven, I created hell

Can you understand, do I make myself clear
Worship the oneness and only me you should fear
Fill your mind, body and soul with valour
Say your prayer my child this is the word of …!

DARK SIDE OF THE LOON

CLASH OF THE TITANS

In the corner of my mind voices are screaming
Sadistic thoughts tell me I am dreaming
No light to comfort just pain and dark
Burnt by a dragon, bit by a shark
A torturing intent masochistically hell bent
Using my soul as a violent vent
Razor blades, shock sticks, shackles, barbwire
A virus, a disease, an intoxicating fire
Atomic death, choking my breath
It feels I've overdosed on heroin and meth
Bubonic plague, a cancerous cell
Rotting flesh, an overwhelming smell
In this kind of reality I've lost my sanity
My body's no longer under force of gravity
So help me God I'm on the dark side
I'm following your rules and laws to abide
The children are dying in this kind of ill
I'm satins' slave; I've no longer free will
My brain is infected that's what I've detected
Psychotic schizophrenia is what I expected
I talk to the moon, pray like a loon
And stir the spirits with a silver spoon
Olanzapine and Aripiprazole a wicked combination
Leave the voices and thoughts with no explanation

Ben Lee Almond

DREAM FACTORY

Welcome to the future, make believe and fun
Everyone's on a buzz nobody's on the run
A land of glory pure friendship's the way
One for all, all for one, this is a happy day
Peace, love and unity
Just the way it's meant to be
Racism gone, prejudice out
Spiritual sanity's, what it's all about
This is the new world it's paradise
I'll tell you once, I'll tell you twice
This monstrous feeling's for everyone
Hate and fear have all gone
Magic enchantment a land of hope
We don't need drugs we don't need dope
C'mon people reach up to the sky
Fresh air, clean streets, nobody will ever lie
Join hands; shout out, I feel really good
Dream factory nightmares
Gone just the way it should

DARK SIDE OF THE LOON

HOLOCAUST DREAMS

Dark, deep, deep, deep dark
Burnt by a dragon, bit by a shark
Sad children crying on a glass covered park
Death and destruction an atomic spark
Walking on razors that's how it seems
I just can't stop these holocaust dreams
I've got bare skin and hostile sunbeams
A blistering body with no antidote creams
A violent virus cancer in me iris
Under attack from murdering pirates
A poisoned mind I can't see I'm blind
Perpetual prison trapped and confined
I'm sick in the brain going insane
I wanna get off this torturing train
Red-hot poker playing cards with a joker
I can't hold on I'm gonna be a croaker
Confused and distorted twisted and contorted
Vicious voices saying my life's aborted
Batons, barbwire an asphyxiating fire
A terrible burning the situation's getting dire
Ripping flesh, razor, wire mesh
Disease ridden babies an infected creche
Hell on earth, pain giving birth
No matter who you are or where's your turf
A blood-sucking leech forced to drink bleach
Negativity and darkness a sadistic breech
Brown bread, dead in the head
Come with me, the grim reaper said

Ben Lee Almond

A BILLION MINDS

Some people say I'm the son Prodigal
Controlled by the moon I'm always methodical
There's methods in my madness, it's easy to say
I talk to the spirits when I meditate and pray

Spreading peace and love this is my special power
A tonic on earth is needed in the darkest hour
I see your wars are wrong, that's why I'm here
So please little darling don't shed no tear

I'll save you from despair, sin, fear and doubt
Take you to the heavens, serenity's all about
A very godly feeling that makes you warm inside
A sensation of tranquillity on this spiritual ride

Inside you all you share one thing that binds
It's a powerful tool as well, its called a billion minds
I'm opening you all up so you share each other's
thoughts
Massive implications but remember what it writes

Everything you touch is magic and soft as silk
And all that you taste is as good as mothers' milk
Listen child don't worry too much 'bout death
Because you're all immortal through your children's
breathe

DARK SIDE OF THE LOON

A DAZE FEROCIOUS

The alien star ship from galaxies bizarre
Bringing magic pills black as blackest tar
Medication time on the lunar ward
I'm a nutty Almond oil one to be adored

My doctor says I come from some other place
Massaging your neck line with aromatherapy base
A spaceman buzzing bringing gifts of love
Quality control you need a little shove

Capturing your mind with my crystal glare
In a daze ferocious you just stand and stare
Bedazzled and bemused you don't understand
The feeling I'm giving you is from a foreign land

Across the darkest seas from interstellar space
Vanishing in an instant without a single trace
Where I've gone to, you can't believe your eyes
I wallow in 27 heaven and dream of deep blue
skies

Prescription drugs versus eating black tar pills
Don't forget my child where you get your thrills

Ben Lee Almond

BLING BLING BLA

Bling Bling Bla but call me Ben
My magic works from the end of a pen
On the paper all over the wall
I kick ass with the way I scroll
Don't even blink you'll miss the ink
I'm a lyrical warlord that's what I think

If you disagree take it from me
I'm a rapper renegade at the top of his tree
Hits and beats outta Rosehill streets
An English Muslim who never cheats
Staetdler to the Bic Bic to the Staetdler
Not a robber and I ain't no dealer

Black, blue and red, I've god a master bed
Radical rhymes flowing outta my head
I'm blessed with a gift, I've got a quick speed shift
I always give the party a massive lift
Put ya ear to the ground you can hear the sound
I'm at full mast and I'm coming around

Up for any test coz I'm the best
Death defiant and I'm full of zest
If ya wanna know what makes me grow
A paper, a pen it's called a biro
This is my rap a lyrical rhyme
I hope you understand how I pass the time

DARK SIDE OF THE LOON

PROS AND CONS

As the golden brown surges through ya blood
You get a warm sensation, really good
Such a nice feeling an instant rush
Better than skunk better than bush

Ya body all tingles it melts through the floor
Floating on a bubble, heaven hardcore
Into the nether world slipping into a dream
A real good buzz strawberries and cream

A godly feeling everything's fine
Ten times better than the rarest wine
The gears all-good and its always strong
But if you think it's gonna last you are wrong

Once you're addicted they weaken it down
Cutting it with crap treating you like a clown
The good feeling's gone you need it to be straight
You've got no money to put food on the plate

Your emotions are battered, weak and frail
Pinned black eyes and a face so pale
You hear no reason you're in denial
Days full of darkness, never a smile

You fall asleep, night or day
When you wake up you've got an instant crave
Pockets are empty you're all in a mix
Your minds only focused on the next fix

An aching body demanding relief
Before you know it you've become a thief

Ben Lee Almond

Digging too much and you've got a blood clot
You're a zombie slave who's lost the plot

DARK SIDE OF THE LOON

HELL A CUBIC CELL

Space and time painfully exist
If you're at the point of slashing your wrist
Feel the thunder, the G force
Blood pumps out and runs its course

Stuck in hell a cubic cell
Two men sharing, what a smell
Get your head down, read a book
Does anybody really give a fuck?

Nowhere to go, nowhere to hide
Can't run from sins, sins to hide
Perfect creation hell on earth
Selling drugs is it really worth

Giving up your kids for moneys sake
Raking it in with a drug dealers rake
Lusting for cash crazy for fame
Now you're to blame coz you played the game

Preston prison, hospital wing
Can't get out, can't do a damn thing?
So take my advice, don't break the law
Else you'll end up in hell with a locked door

Ben Lee Almond

STEAL THE SHOW

Purple horizons melting away
I wish for the same every day
The nighttime skyline fading slow
You can see the last magical glow

The next day, is it red, yellow or pink
A marvellous beauty is what I think
Colours all merged mingling together
After a scorching day this is perfect weather

Who controls this mystical wonder?
The same God who brings us thunder
Lightning winds and sometimes snow
Don't try to master it coz it's not your show

DARK SIDE OF THE LOON

EYE SPY

Camera, camera, lets play eye spy
Christopher's story a murdering lie
No crime was committed is what they said
A healthy strong paratrooper ended up dead

Injustice is wrong so what about it
Government corruption they don't give a shit
Lots of lies all the time
Caught on film you can see the crime

So what you gonna do Mr. Blunket
Christopher's blood all of you drunk it
Janet and family want the truth
Not to mention Christopher's tooth

In the van did they gas his face?
Clothes and canisters destroyed in a race
Blair and government do you think we're fools
We've seen the truth and it's a powerful tool

Nasty policemen they all denied
A set up scenario when they got tried
We know what happened, its plain to see
The truth must out to set Christopher free

Ben Lee Almond

DEATH OR JAIL

Don't be a fool smack'll bring you to your knees
Steer well clear of the heroin disease
You're going crazy for the powder brown
Why can't you see it's bringing you down?

Everyone can see you're an addicted fool
You need some education so go back to fucking
school
It's your own fault when your willy turns dud
You're just a waster with infected blood

No money, no care just half asleep
This terrible affliction catches all the sheep
It's easy to say your brain's at the boil
Injecting death a slave to the foil

The opium God has captured your soul
A bag of bones, time's taken its toll
I can't believe you steal off your friends
Burning all your bridges the deception never ends

Sooner or later you'll be doing time
Do you really want a life of crime?
Your mind is weak your body is frail
You've got two choices death or jail

DARK SIDE OF THE LOON

A POSITIVE POEM

Warm sun beams, tranquil streams
Trustful teams and peaceful dreams
Happy children playing love and light spraying
Paradise on earth that's what I'm saying

No disease just flourishing trees
Clear skies of blue birds and bees
Serenity's here cast away fears
There's no need to shed any more tears

This magic is real for everyone to feel
Nobody's worried about the next meal
Enchantment hope no need for dope
Heavens at the bottom of every slope

Twinkling stars no crashing cars
Alcohol is banned at all of the bars
There's no crime but plenty of time
Have faith the water will turn to wine

Ben Lee Almond

THE GNARLED TREE

Ever see a tree in a field on its own
Solitary, singular and all alone

Gnarled, twisted, unique and strange
A lonesome wizard quite out of range

A log roll, a totem pole
Wicked and wild with a wooden soul

Who put it there in the weather to bear?
And showed it affection and loving care

A farmer, a friend, who did spend
Time on a tree from beginning to end

DARK SIDE OF THE LOON

ALREADY DEAD

Mixed up, confused, a religious geek
A tobacco giant now who's the freak?
Don't look at me like I'm some kind of strange
Maybe it's yourself you need to rearrange

Am I Polish, Jamaican or Serb?
If I'm asleep please don't disturb
Cancerous cell infectious wound
Now I've got your attention, into me you've tuned

Listen fool you're nobody big
I've got summat to tell you, this you've gotta dig
I've sussed the Bible and the Koran
A fiery Aries I'm an Easter day man

A leader, a king, a God some say
Coz you've never seen the mad way I pray
Cosmic powers and a Ouiji board
Trust me son I'm on a psycho ward

Interstellar travel on spaceship trains
I use ESP and I've gotta lotta brains
A voodoo doll and voices in me head
Nowt can touch me I'm already dead

Its easy, see, just think of 27
And every time you can reach heaven

Ben Lee Almond

EYES WIDE SHUT

It infiltrates society it targets anyone
Sirens calling, this is a warning,
Beware of the heroin bomb
When it came to town this golden brown

Nobody seemed to wear a frown
But after the weeks there were bony cheeks
This is how the opium god speaks
Misery and sadness children slaves
Hundreds and thousands of early graves

Pinned black eyes, no disguise
Thieving and robbing, telling lies
You keep on slipping down the bottomless hole
It's got a tight grip this mind control

Infecting blood cells and killing your brain
A one way ticket to suffering and pain
You wanna stop but where's your will
You keep searching for the first cheap thrill

The buzz is gone it don't work no more
Just to be normal and survive the war
Chasing a rush that just won't come
Injecting death is really dumb

Negative thoughts rule the mind
Eyes wide shut you may as well be blind

DARK SIDE OF THE LOON

RATIONAL MINDS WON'T BELIEVE

I know you don't believe me
A rational mind says this

There is no God above a man
It's either hit or miss

Black or white, there is no grey
When you die you're gone

Reboot your depth of thinking
And tune into the one

Once you feel the truth my friend
You'll laugh till you are spare

Now you know your life is safe
It's been in God's care

Ben Lee Almond

I LOVE YOU

Memories aren't enough for me
Your face in reality, I need to see
To touch to taste
You smell so sweet
Sweeping privets on your front street

Janet Alder you are mine
When you are around, I feel fine
Talking, looking, making love
Heaven sent a gift from above

Two hearts, the same pure fusion
No bad vibes, no confusion
Many moons we have spent apart
Dark and dreary was my heart

You speak to me, honest and free
The lights still there, will always be
You nurtured me back to health
You've brought my life such a wealth

You're worth much more than all the books
Much more than any object looks
Material life, I've left it be
All I need is you for me

DARK SIDE OF THE LOON

A LIQUID BLACK

I think war is crazy especially in Iraq
Coz Americas just pinching a liquid, very black
Shooting innocent people, missiles in your house
Rodents in the testing zone, better treatment to a
mouse
Weapons of mass destruction are nowhere to be
seen
An excuse to nick the oil, Bush, you're really mean
Muslims sussed you out so defy your military jargon
Controlling all their land you drive a hard bargain
The public in our countries don't want our armies
there
You're letting us down too much, this cruelty's hard
to bear
So listen Bush and Blair take it from me
Withdraw the monstrous tanks and leave that
country free

Ben Lee Almond

SANDMAN'S LAIR

Hell on earth, this is nightmare land
You've got bare feet and glass is where you stand
You try to run but don't go anywhere
This is a dark dream you better be aware
Dungeons and dragons, demons and pain
The twilight zone you're going insane
A wizard, a witch, hobgoblin, a ghoul
This is the sandman's lair so don't be a fool
Take your soul, Freddy Kruger thinks he can
And you better watch out for the bogie man
I'm telling you now the Candy Man and his bees
Scare you to death and bring you to your knees
Your mind's on fire, a burning sensation
In this type of dream there's no explanation
Everything's backwards or it seems to be
Don't eat cheese at night, take it from me
Lashing your brain right to the extreme
You wish you could wake up from this torturing
dream

DARK SIDE OF THE LOON

MR BLAIR WOTCHA SMOKIN'

Mr. Blair you're so unfair
We can see, you don't really care
You've lied to us more than once
You should resign, you arrogant ponce

Giving the police a license to kill
Pushing fast the terrorist bill
Instilling fear to get your voters
Dissecting society into more than quarters

Thousands die off just one lie
Parentless children left to cry
So what can you say to England's youth?
When you can't own up or tell the truth

Don't look back just look ahead
You must think we're dead in the head
Death's in custody and a violent war
Put them behind you and close the door

No way man, well never forget
You killed our loved ones with no regret
We're not all sheep some of us care
Blood for oil that's hardly fair

You murdered Christopher because he was black
You're doing the same for oil in Iraq
Mr. Blair you must be smoking crack
This back to front government is totally whack

CE 81 DRAW

I'm a patient on ward 18
It's the weirdest place I've ever been
First of all they get you addicted
Tablets galore my ideas conflicted

See they shouldn't have given me Ativan
Now I'm addicted a dependant man
They wiped me off so sudden so soon
Now I rage round like some kind of loon

They put you on they take you off
They've turned me into a tablet boff
Olanzapine, Depokote, Respiredone too
All these meds make me feel blue

Lorazepam is all I need
After all I've stopped smoking weed
Temazepam, Valium my body craves
An addiction to downers a pathway paves

DARK SIDE OF THE LOON

OPEN SESAMIE SPELLCASTER

Hobgoblins eye, electric sky
Elfish tongue, a werewolf's cry
Pixie ring, David's sling
Dwarfs axe, blood of a king
Oarks hair, fur of a bear
Snakes venom, a witch's stare
Voodoo bones, ancient stones
Darkness and chaos, hybrid clones

Tranquil tunes, mystic runes
Magical spoons, 27 moons
Flying Cars, Rivers on mars
Crystal balls, spells in jars
Exquisite screams, nightmarish dreams
Mammoths' tusk, laser beams
Alcohol and meth, giants' breath
Dinosaurs tooth, Black Death

Dirty deeds, weeds and seeds
Fairy's and trolls, interbreeds
Cosmic powers, psychedelic flowers
Liquid space, holocaust hours
Sorcerer's soul, wizard's staff
I bear the words of Allah's craft
Shimmering fire, illuminating ice
Captain Zappa and Almond spice

Crocodiles' scales, dragons' claw
Knock, knock, knock now OPEN DAMN DOOR

Ben Lee Almond

DRY YOUR EYES MATE

Demons digging deep in my soul
Sooner or later Ill be paying the reaper's toll
Welcoming and open to negativity
This death spirit just won't leave me be

Ghouls and witches comforting me
I'm under a spell no longer free
What will happen, now death is so dark
Sad children crying on a glass covered park

This is the end as I have been cursed
I've been declared dead, I'm trapped in a hearse
The light has all gone, my eyes are now closed
Deep in this casket in the morgue I am froze

DARK SIDE OF THE LOON

INSECURITY OPPOSITES ATTRACT

I am dark but you are bright
I am wrong and you are right
I am slow but you are fast
You are first, I am last
I make a frown, you a smile
I am an inch, you are a mile
I give in, you always try
I'm drowning, yeah, you fly
I'm unequipped, you're sorted
You're getting started, I'm aborted
I'm sloppy, you're real neat
I'm bitter, you're so sweet
I ain't got a clue, you've got it sussed
I'm sluggish, you've got thrust
I'm a tied knot, you a perfect line
I feel ill, you feel fine
I'm a nightmare, you a nice dream
I've gone sour, you're fresh cream
I'm real lazy, you're up and ready
I'm so shaky, you're rock steady
I start to crumble, you just bond
I've gotta stick, you gotta wand
I'm an addictive, you've got will
I'm boring, you're a thrill

Ben Lee Almond

TEARS ARE HOLY

My tears are like diamonds
Falling into space
Echoing insignificance
Vanishing without a trace
Rippling through the air
But then they fade away
Leaving me behind
To cry another day

DARK SIDE OF THE LOON

ANCIENT WHISPERS

I hear the voices of the ancients
Whispering in my ear
When I told the doctors
They said, "YOU MUST STAY HERE"
Six months down the line
No cure or prevention
I hear the voices of the ancients
They've become my only redemption

Ben Lee Almond

COCKTAIL RAMPAGE

Knocking 'em down and knocking 'em back
I'm up at dawn and I'm up for the crack
Joking, jesting, jolly all the way
Coz my fucking bar man's up all day
All through the night he's open already
Go and get the cocktails and let's get steady
Tequila, rum and Jamaican brandy
A little bit of whisky would be handy
Jungle drinks, its cocktails galore
We get real ratted but we still want more
Say no to Charlie, I'm on an alcoholic high
A spiritual feeling, I'll tell you no lie
A clear juice drink with lashings of rum
This party's kicking, everyone can come
Drinks in each hand take 'em in twos
Cocktail rampage, forget the blues

DARK SIDE OF THE LOON

ABOLISHMENT

It's a crazy world we're in, most chasing a rush
Blinded by reality they develop a hot and cold flush
Disconnected from realisation, drugged up to the
max
Tough love and knowledge is what this country
lacks

I'm sick of being sorry for these zombies with a lust
I'd like to offer salvation but don't know who to trust
Lying, cheating, thieving, no good down and out
bums
Do they really realise the grim reaper always
comes?

Smacked up, cracked in, speeding and tamazified
Badness taking over, reach for your spiritual side
Boy you're in a mess you're just skin and bones
You need nourishment child, I hear your belly
groans

Asleep with a burning fag, proper on a mong
Look at the state you're in, man, this has to be
wrong
You're not living your life you're just wasting away
Stopping is really easy, just meditate and pray

Do you think its cool an addict to the foil?
Why don't you wake up from the abyss of turmoil?
I pray for the abolishment of heroin, crack and
speed
This glorious country knows they're three things we
don't really need

Ben Lee Almond

BOOK HAT STONES

Eternal keys, objects of desire
The wizard's stones, a power none higher
A pyramid star and a red moon
But only with the right book do they sing in tune

A dark ancient voodoo polyglot bible
Passed down the ages, wisdom from the tribal
Cosmic encryptions, forgotten descriptions
Curing the universe with natural prescriptions

A caldron of dreams, exquisite screams
The waterfall of life and tranquil streams
Book and stones to the magic hat
A dragons maze, a delicate bat

Thorns in mind but I don't frown
When I wear the flower patterned golden crown

DARK SIDE OF THE LOON

THE EARTH AND THE FIRE

The earth is scorched by the raging fire
Live flames burning higher and higher
Blistering the grass, tormenting the trees
Taking no prisoners, no birds no bees

This death light zapping everything in its way
A terrifying delight, burns night and day
Out of control, but precisely so it seems
Nothing escapes this violence and direct sunbeams

Penetrative, bursting through all living things
A hostility rampage is what this fire brings
A starry colossal, striking, sizzling all
How can you stop the *dograts* who creates the
blazing wall?

Peace at last, the inferno is no more
But after the mayhem, earth's won this war
She's a wicked nature, for she has very deep roots
The mother earth gives birth to newly sprung
shoots

After a while her magic spreads to buds
As quickly as that, there's a whole new type of
woods
It seems nothing can stop this fast growing spree
Jesus nor Mohammad, nor you nor me

God and the elements are a force unmatched
Earth forgives fire coz she's only scratched

A SNITCH IN TIME SAVES CRIME

Bush and Blair, what a pair
How they've still got any hair
When will England think on its own?
Instead of trusting Bush's clone
America's had its racial war
Now they're pushing it at our door
We've already got racial tension
All stirred up not to mention
Suicide this and Muslim that
Nobody trusts Bush the mental brat
Going round all foreign land
Dealing out punishment hand by hand
When will it stop, is there an end
Religious sects driven round the bend
Well Bush and Blair hear us say
Islamic religion is here to stay
Was here a time long ago
So some facts you should know
Chemical gas, metal sticks and shackles
Should never be the way to win your battles
Don't be silly, don't be a fool
Mr. Blair you went to private school
The BNP stole lots of your votes
The people who voted are hungry as goats
Hungry with hatred of other people's race
But for you it's hard to face
Some people didn't want you in power
So voted for anyone else in your finest hour

DARK SIDE OF THE LOON

DIRTY DEED

Speed is a stimulant, it makes you go fast
It's so dangerous, please don't give it a blast
Corroding your brain and blackening your teeth
So you can't enjoy succulent lamb and beef

You can't sleep, insomniac even counting sheep
And there's no help from little Bo peep
Manically depressed and you wonder why
Denying it to yourself, boy, it makes me cry

You can't eat a thing, you're just wasting away
Your body needs vitamins every single day
An addicted slave to amphetamine rubbish
I talk to help you realise so you become
discouraged

Drained and knackered out until you get a hit
Can't you see the cycle or don't you give a shit?
Your life is in a mess your house is in a state
The whiz is twisting you up and making you irate

Your eyes are always bulging, you're talking in a
rush
You need to calm right down and the pattern to
adjust
I see you're in trouble with the filthy fuzz
It's so very sad you're just doing it for a buzz

Ben Lee Almond

FINDERS KEEPERS

Finders keepers, losers weepers
Spiritual sanity's not for sleepers
Lessons in life are learned through strife
Sometimes we need to be cut by the knife

Friends come and go but love is forever
Trust that God's with you through stormy weather
Bo Lozoffs wisdom spreads love and peace
The teaching's worldwide, will never cease

Sweet sunshine and beautiful clear blue skies
Spiritual warriors with knowledge in our eyes
Brothers and sisters, side by side
In it together we're on the same ride

United in harmony, tranquillity rules
Spiritual sanity's taught in our schools
A new world order across every border
Every living creature has pure clean water

Love giving birth on everybody's turf
A state of pristine ecstasy all over mother earth

DARK SIDE OF THE LOON

A BIRO DEPLETION

The paper, the paper, clean, white and crisp
The ink makes mistakes like a stumbling lisp
After completion of a biro depletion
A work of art with no restriction

Words, letters, letters and words
Consonants, vowels, adjectives, verbs
Poems, rhymes, raps and beats
Anything to get off the battle-ridden streets

Gonna use my brain before I go insane
Full steam ahead like a poetry train
Ripping up the page in a lyrical rage
A dream supreme busting outta my cage

An Anchor blue all the way through
I prophesise and it comes true
The time is now someway or somehow
I've got morals, I don't beg nor bow

Listen to my rhyme, tell me what you think
Because Bling Bling Bla's the King of ink

A SECRET PLACE

Lush grass, blue skies, beautiful golden sand
Paradise on earth made by God's hand
Crystal clear water cascading into heaven
To find this secret place turn right at cloud 27
A fountain of youth everyone's real tranquil
We've all found Zion and to God we're all so
thankful
There's a hidden trail and an ancient tale
Walk the trail, hear the tale, wet your mind from the
Holy Grail
Enter a realm of unity, brothers and sisters unite
All the colours of the rainbow exquisite to the sight
Every meals a banquette, you'll dream it then it's
there
Exotic tastes aplenty, positively in the air
Nobody's a stranger here our minds interconnect
In such a sacred place it's what you would expect
Such a blissful feeling, serenity giving birth
A state of pure ecstasy we've never dreamt of on
the earth

DARK SIDE OF THE LOON

SWEET DREAMS

In this world of lust, fame and greed
You're the only thing I truly need
A treasure even God can't measure
Loving you Janet it's such a pleasure

You're real, you're love I feel
Before you I bow and kneel
Awe inspiring, so satisfying
For you I just keep on trying

The earth and fire we're bound to meet
You are the colour in my clean sheet
The perfume in the sweetest flower
I yearn for you, every second, minute, hour

Sparkling silver, glittering gold
Over you they have no hold
So come to me my warrior queen
And through the night we will sweetly dream

Ben Lee Almond

BO LOZOFF

Spiritual mysteries to explore
Into the nether world hardcore
A state of ecstasy, clean and pure
Enlightenment for all of this I'm sure

Meditations and religion help pacify the heart
Spreading loving kindness is a good way to start
Only one God you have his guarantee
Be good to your brothers, he will set you free

If you're somewhere but don't know where you are
The lord will show you the way, is it so bizarre?
Grief, pain, loneliness and fear
In the afterlife they're only words to here

Spiritual sanity this is a natural high
Clouds in a boundless sky

DARK SIDE OF THE LOON

MASTERING THE VOICES

I try to listen to the voices in my head
Some of them saying I'm going to be dead
Spirits come and spirits go
Why they chose me I really don't know

Is it really real these thought of death
All day long even after every breath?
So what I do is play their game
And I coax these voices down the lane

I take them to places, in my brain
In doing this I drive them insane
They can't break through to my mind
Someone weaker they will have to find

I block them out with a God force field
The voices start lagging is what is revealed
Evil whispers, now you're in trouble
I've created a cure; it's an oxygen bubble

Surrounded by love, family and friends
My power just grows, it never ends
Spiritual sanity has helped me to cope
But at the time I had given up hope

Books and prayer but meditation is the key
These tools are there for you and for me
Voices and thoughts, now leave me alone
Coz Bling Bling Bla's sat on his own throne

Ben Lee Almond

DREAM MACHINE

In the deepest depths of an Almond mind
Planets and star charts you will find
But don't be fooled they make no sense
I'm from zillions of miles across the fence

A time traveller from galaxies afar
I come to earth; I saw your door ajar
We use E.S.P from where I live
I can hear your thoughts, don't call me a div

Your earth is small compared to mine
One sun, nine planets, all in a line
We have no sun where I'm from
We don't have bullets or a bomb

All of my people live in harmony
Powers abundant, we have oils from sea
Solar power and wind turbines
You're catching up, a sign of the times

When your sun runs out, you will die
I can help and I won't cry
I've hidden something in your ocean
If this technology is put into motion

It will create dark and light
Making day and making night
It's so easy my people, advance
You have to find it, here's your chance

Its hidden good, it's hidden well
It makes heaven, it makes hell

DARK SIDE OF THE LOON

Diamonds, rainbows, money too
But it's for everyone not just you

It can be found I know it can
It'll save the animals; it'll save the man
Wars will be a thing of the past
Just turn it on, give it a blast

If your people can find my machine
You will be stuck in a dream
Eternal life I give to you
There's no such colour as the colour blue

Human beings all equal, all free
Peace and love, the way it should be
So philosophers, scientists, star boffs too
I'll give you a chance, a little clue

My gizmos the size of a grain of sand
Look to the sea, its not on land
A miracle worker is my gadget
Life for all it makes magic

I'll tell you once, I'll tell you twice
In my world there's no blind mice

Ben Lee Almond

BROTHERS AND SISTERS

Please almighty lord take care of my brothers and
sisters
Make not drugs and sex rule our children's minds

I pray to you, offering myself as sacrifice
Have mercy on the world, cure it, heal it

Let your compassion be upon us
Have faith in all, peace will be triumphant

I feel your power and divine presence
Let positivity be abundant, clear skies of blue

Flood mankind with love, let serenity flourish
Now is the time for your healing hand

Enlightenment for all knowledge, wisdom and truth

DARK SIDE OF THE LOON

I am 28 years old and was born in Blackburn and raised in Burnley. I have been in and out of a lot of different institutions since the age of six. The first time I was admitted was to the Mary Burbury unit at Burnley general hospital. I have been to prison a few times, a few children's homes and many different types of wards and psychiatric units.

After spending so much time in these places, I started to write poems about how I felt and what was going through my mind. I made lots of them flow and rhyme with long dark descriptive words, which reflected where my head was at the time. I documented my experience with schizophrenic affective disorder and the results are profound.

I was heavily into drugs, which took me to dark places. Some of my poems explain the negativity that they create and the nasty world around them when you take them. I have seen many people in prisons and hospitals with drug-induced psychosis and have been through it myself. I would love these poems in particular to serve as a deterrent for anyone even thinking of trying drugs.

Some of these poems are here to give you an insight into drugs and the affects on mental health disorders that people experience, myself included. This book was mainly written as I was moved from one institution to the next and became a big part in my self-counselling, which has helped me greatly along the road.

Lightning Source UK Ltd.
Milton Keynes UK
UKOW04f0848050315

247264UK00001B/27/P